TIME FOR KIDS READERS

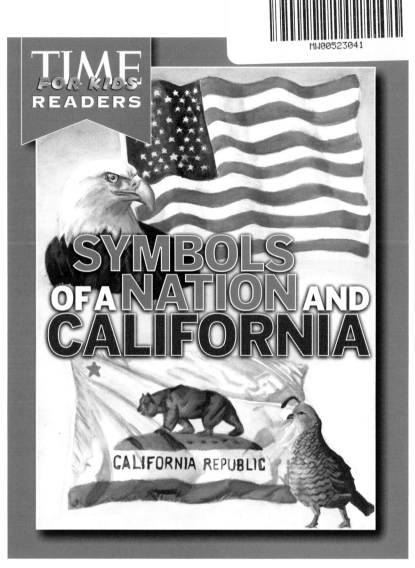

SYMBOLS OF A NATION AND CALIFORNIA

CALIFORNIA REPUBLIC

by Elaine Israel

Harcourt
SCHOOL PUBLISHERS

Orlando   Austin   New York   San Diego   Toronto   London

Visit *The Learning Site!*
www.harcourtschool.com

It's the day of the big baseball game. In the stadium, thousands of people wait for the shout "Play ball!"

But first, the crowd stands. A color guard marches out onto the field, carrying the state flag and the flag of the United States. All join in the singing of "The Star-Spangled Banner."

The flag and the song are symbols of the United States. They stand for democracy and freedom.

The United States has many symbols. Some of our statues and buildings are symbols that remind us of important people and events. Still other symbols say, "We are Americans. We take pride in our country."

The United States is often represented by the figure of Uncle Sam. For almost 200 years he has appeared on postage stamps, posters, and even food labels.

Uncle Sam

Baseball players honor the U.S. flag by singing "The Star-Spangled Banner."

Golden Times

Californians have symbols that celebrate California's land, animals, and history.

Besides symbols, California has a nickname. What nickname do you think would tell the world about California? What things are Californians proud of?

California's state flag

They are proud of their sunny weather. In the spring, they are proud of their fields of golden poppies—the state flower. They are also proud that the gold rush took place in their hills.

California was given the official nickname, "The Golden State," in 1968.

These are some more of California's symbols:

State dance—West Coast swing

State folk dance—square dancing

State insect—dogface butterfly

State rock—serpentine

The golden poppy is California's state flower.

Sing Out!

Some symbols, such as songs, are heard but not seen. The national anthem, or official song, of the United States is "The Star-Spangled Banner." It was written by Francis Scott Key, an American who was on a British ship during the War of 1812. The British were firing rockets at Fort McHenry in the harbor of Baltimore, Maryland. Key watched proudly all night as the United States flag kept flying through the fire and smoke and "the rockets' red glare."

The Golden State is so big that it once had more than one state song. But in 1988 "I Love You, California" became the official state song. A California storekeeper named F. B. Silverwood wrote the words. The music was composed by Alfred Frankenstein, who once led the Los Angeles Symphony Orchestra.

While watching the rockets firing over Fort McHenry, Francis Scott Key (standing) wrote the first lines of "The Star-Spangled Banner" on the back of a letter.

A Few Good Words

There are many different kinds of people in the United States. Some people like our nation's official motto, In God We Trust. Others prefer the motto that is on the Great Seal, the official emblem of the United States. It is written in Latin. The motto on the seal, E Pluribus Unum, means "out of many, one." This motto reminds us that the United States was created from 13 colonies.

The Great Seal of the United States

California's motto is *Eureka*, a Greek word meaning "I have found it." Thousands of years ago, that's what a Greek scientist cried out when he found a way to figure out the volume of gold.

"Eureka!" is what California gold miners shouted when they found gold in 1848. *Eureka* has been the official California motto since 1963.

Gold nuggets

These lucky men found gold! They carry the gold in the pan on the man's head.

State seals also show how important a state is. California's Great Seal tells the state's colorful history. The seal shows a grizzly bear, a goddess, a miner, mountains, the word *Eureka*, ships, and 31 stars.

The Great Seal of California

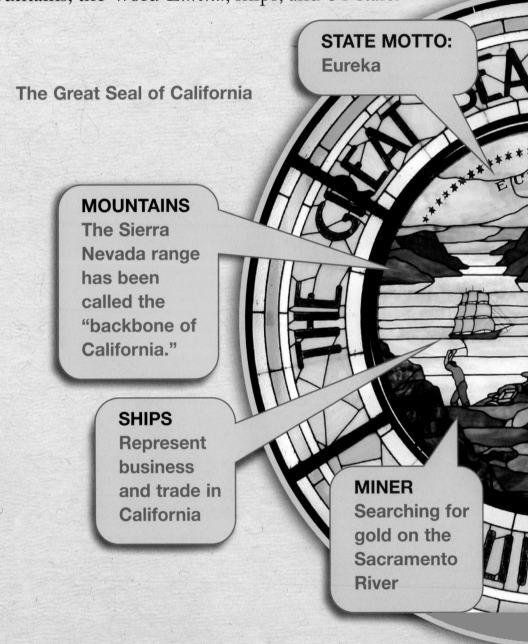

STATE MOTTO:
Eureka

MOUNTAINS
The Sierra Nevada range has been called the "backbone of California."

SHIPS
Represent business and trade in California

MINER
Searching for gold on the Sacramento River

The Great Seal, made of colorful stained glass, is in a ceiling near the rotunda—a round, open area—of the state capitol building in Sacramento.

31 STARS
The number of states in the United States when California joined the Union in 1850

ROMAN GODDESS
The goddess of wisdom, Minerva

GRIZZLY BEAR
This large and powerful creature, now no longer found in California, is the state animal.

Home Sweet Home

In a democracy, the citizens elect the people in the national and state governments. So the places in which those governments meet may be the most important of all buildings. The Capitol in Washington, D.C., where the United States Congress meets, is a symbol of our democracy.

In Sacramento, the capital of California, the capitol building looks like the U.S. Capitol building. For example, the California state capitol has a rotunda with a dome, just like the U.S. Capitol.

It took 14 years to build the California capitol. It was finished in 1874. The capitol has been through many changes over the years.

United States Capitol

The California capitol is a working museum. By taking a tour of this building, visitors can learn a lot about California's past and present.

Hail the Quail

The bald eagle—a large, majestic bird that flies high above the trees—is the national bird of the United States. With its large and powerful wingspan, it is able to soar. The bald eagle stands for our country's strength and freedom.

In 1782 the bald eagle became the national bird of the United States. At that time it was placed on the Great Seal of our country.

The California quail, which runs quickly through brush, is the state bird of California. It lives in coveys—groups that sometimes have up to 200 birds. The quail, also called the valley quail, is often seen on the Pacific coast. This bird stands for Californians' strength and ability to adapt easily to their surroundings.

The California quail is smaller than a pigeon. Its coloring helps it hide in its environment.

I Love You, California

written by F. B. Silverwood
music composed by Alfred Frankenstein

I love you, California, you're the greatest state of all.
I love you in the winter, summer,
spring, and in the fall.
I love your fertile valleys;
your dear mountains I adore.
I love your grand old ocean
and I love her rugged shore.

CHORUS: Where the snow-crowned Golden Sierras
Keep their watch o'er the valleys bloom,
It is there I would be in our land by the sea,
Ev'ry breeze bearing rich perfume.
It is here nature gives of her rarest.
It is Home Sweet Home to me,
And I know when I die I shall breathe my last sigh
For my sunny California.

The High Sierra, some of the highest peaks of the Sierra Nevada, run through Yosemite National Park.